Walki

to

Abbeys, Castles & Churches

by

J. Brian Beadle

This book is dedicated to Chris.
Without whose navigational skills
I would still be out there!

The Author and Publisher of this guide do not accept any responsibility for the accuracy of the general information, tours, routes, timetables etc. All routes were open at the time of publication. Any suggested routes should be treated with respect and all precautions taken before setting out. Any person using information contained in this book do so entirely at their own risk.

First published in Great Britain in 1995 by Trailblazer Publishing (Scarborough)

www.trailblazerbooks.co.uk

ISBN 1 899004 07 6

Trailblazer Publishing (Scarborough)
Stoneways
South End
Burniston
Scarborough. YO13 0HP

MAPS
The maps in this book are not to scale and are for guidance only. They do not accurately portray the right of way. It is the readers responsibility not to stray from the right of way and it is strongly advised that you take an Ordnance Survey map with you on the walk.

WARNING
Whilst every effort has been made for accuracy neither the publisher nor the author bear responsibility for the alteration, closure or portrayal of rights of way in this book. It is the readers responsibility not to invade private land or stray from the public right of way. All routes in the book should be treated with respect and all precautions taken before setting out. Take food, drink, an emergency whistle and warm clothing with you and tell someone where you are going and your expected time of return. Any person using information in this book does so at their own risk.

ISBN 1 899004 07 6

CONTENTS

WHARRAM PERCY

*W*harram Percy is a deserted medieval village. Most of the inhabitants were wiped out by the Black Death around 1350 leaving only a few surviving farm workers. The main feature of Wharram Percy is St. Martin's Church. The earliest church was built of timber and kop (clay mixed with straw, gravel and sand). This was replaced by a small stone church with the chancel being added later. The tower being built in the 12th century. Population was growing in the area around Wharram Percy and north and south aisles were added, only to be demolished around 1500. The blocked off arches can still be seen. Materials from demolition were re-used, hence the 12th century arch and some Saxon remains. The church was still being used in 1949 when the lead was stolen from the roof and it became a ruin.

FACT FILE
Distance - 8 miles (13km)
Time - 4 hours
Maps - OS Landranger 100
Start - Thixendale Village. GR 842611
Terrain - Field side paths over the Wolds
Parking - Roadside at Thixendale
Refreshments - Pub & Cafe at Thixendale

The Route

1. Parking is scarce in Thixendale village so please park with due respect for residents, farm entrances and other walkers. Set off in a westerly direction with the pub at your back towards Water Dale. Approaching the end of the village follow the Wolds Way sign on the right up a wide chalk road. At the top of the hill bear left keeping to the Wolds Way, crossing a stile onto Cow Wold.

2. Follow the path around the edge of the field which eventually turns sharp right and soon descends into the valley. Go through the gate then bear right following the waymarked path up the other side of the valley. Cross over the stile heading for a thicket a little further along.

3. Pass through the thicket, bear right and follow the Wolds Way sign directing you along the edge of Cow Wold. In 1½ miles bear left to leave the Wolds Way. Walk along the edge of Deep Dale following the sign to Wharram Percy.
You will notice the ruin of St. Martin's Church nestling in the hollow at the end of the dale.

4. On reaching the deserted village and church ruin cross the stile to enter the site near the fish pond, then through a kissing gate to the churchyard. The ruin and site are now owned by English Heritage. Inside the church you will find plaques giving a well documented history of this ancient building and the surrounding settlement.

5. Leave Wharram Percy the same way that you came, then in about 1½ miles turn left at the waymark for CW (The Centenary Way). Keep on the grassy path to the ruins of Wold House then join a chalk road. In approximately ½ mile follow the waymark right along the field edge and eventually over a stile and into Raisdale.

6. The views from this point are unusual with steep sided, flat bottomed valleys everywhere. Turn left over a stile and follow the sheep track which leads to the road. At the road turn right to return to Thixendale. Although the village is only small it does boast a cafe and a public house for refreshment.

The church in its heyday served four nearby villages. Thixendale being the only survivor. Imagine walking from the village twice a day on Sundays! It was last used in 1949 and deteriorated badly when the lead was stolen from the roof. The church has many interesting features, make sure you see them all.
Whilst at Wharram Percy have a look at the rest of the site of this important medieval village. Many foundations have been excavated and are labelled. There is also a fishpond which you passed on the way in. There are many deserted villages on the Yorkshire Wolds but none are as interesting as Wharram Percy.

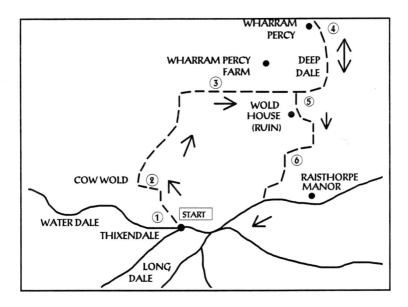

ESKDALE AND DANBY CASTLE
Fairy Cross Plain, Fryup and Duck Bridge. Standing stones, burial cairns and funeral circles. All are places of interest and intrigue on this superb walk from Eskdale to Danby Rigg. This time the walk takes us to Danby Castle and over the magnificent Duck Bridge.

Danby Castle had royal connections as Catherine Parr, the last of Henry VIII's wives lived there. Built by William Latimer in the early 14th century it is one of the finest quadrangular castles in the country. It replaced a simpler type of castle at Castleton and was built not only for defence but for the comfort of its occupants. There are still two rooms of the original in use. One is used as a courtroom, the Danby Court Leet, a rare medieval manor court. It has a high backed 17th century oak judge's seat. The other room is used as a meeting room to discuss court business.

When Latimer built Danby castle it ruined him and when he died in 1335 he was not buried for a month because of a shortage of money. The estate eventually passed to the Nevilles of Raby whose arms decorate the front of the courthouse. The castle is now part of Lord Downes Wykeham estate and is being restored by English Heritage.

FACT FILE
Distance - 7½ miles (12km).
Time - 3 hours.
Maps - OS Landranger 94
OS Outdoor Leisure 27
Start - The Moors Centre, Danby. GR 717084.
Terrain - Good wide Bridleways. A little rough in places over Danby Rigg.
Parking - Good free car park at the Moors Centre.
Refreshments - Cafe at the Moors Centre. Pub slightly off route at Ainthorpe.
Public Transport - Moorsbus on summer Sundays and Bank Holidays from Pickering, timetable from 0439 770173. Train from Whitby to Danby station, details from BR.

The Route
1. Starting from the Moors Centre car park at Danby turn left. In less than a mile take the bridleway sign on the right along the drive to Crag Farm. Where the drive goes sharp left to the farm go straight ahead along a wide grassy path, then straight ahead across a rough field to a wooden footpath signpost.

2. Turn right at the signpost along a wide path. This path traverses many fields, there are some small yellow waymarks painted on the gates. Keep straight ahead at all times passing the seemingly deserted Foresters Lodge, eventually meeting a wide green lane to exit onto the road at the farm at Stonebeck Gate.

3. Go left here up the hill to Fairy Cross Plain cottage. Take the bridleway signed to the right through the gate opposite the cottage. Cross the field to another gate then head uphill slightly right to another gate to join a wide track onto the moor.

4. At the road turn right enjoying the views along Great Fryup Dale to the right. A short downhill section of quiet road into Little Fryup Dale brings you to a junction. Take the 'Bridleway to Ainthorpe' route as signed to the left. This is a good if tiring climb onto Danby Rigg.

5. Follow the obvious wide bridleway over the Rigg enjoying good views towards Danby Dale on the left. If you feel an atmosphere across the Rigg it could be from the many burial places nearby. You will see a large standing stone and a circle of stones near to the path. It is said to be connected with ancient funeral rites. Enter if you dare!

6. Continue along to exit the moor via a gate then a path to a quiet road. If you wish to refresh yourself turn left to the Fox & Hounds Inn at Ainthorpe, a short walk down the hill. Otherwise turn right. At the junction in less than a mile turn left, but not before taking a look at the remains of Danby Castle on your right.

7. Soon you arrive at Duck Bridge, a well preserved packhorse bridge which was rebuilt many years ago by a Mr Duck, hence the name. Walk over the bridge and in a few yards turn left to return to the car park. I recommend a visit to the Moors Centre which is housed in an old shooting lodge and is full of information, not to mention toilets and a cup of tea!

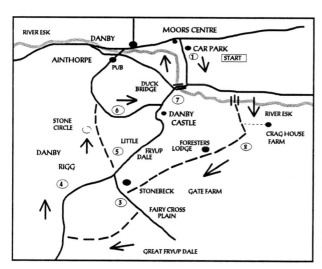

Not far from Danby Castle is Duck Bridge, an old packhorse bridge that spans the River Esk. Near the castle were old iron furnaces that were worked by Danish crofters before the Norman Conquest. But perhaps the most outstanding feature of the walk is the view from the edge of Danby High Moor along Fryup Dale.

ROUTE 3

THE MONASTIC CELL OF HACKNESS

The ancient village of Hackness lies in a tranquil valley surrounded by wooded hills. It boasts a fine church which has several Norman arches. Inside the church are the remains of an ancient cross perhaps connected with the monastic cell which was founded in AD 680 by St. Hilda, Abbess of Whitby. This settlement was destroyed by marauding Vikings less than a hundred years later. A second foundation was formed in 1078 when the charm and beauty of Hackness was home to an order of Monks.

FACT FILE
Distance - 7 miles (11km)
Time - 3 hours
Maps - OS Landranger 101
OS Outdoor Leisure 27
Start - Lowdales/Highdales road end, Hackness. GR 967906
Terrain: Mainly grassy tracks, rough in places
Parking - Roadside at Hackness
Refreshments: The Moorcock Inn at Langdale End
Public Transport: Countryside Bus Services Tel: 0723 870790 for details

The Route

1. The walk starts at the junction of the road to Low Dales/High Dales adjacent to the bridge over the beck in Hackness village. Walk through the village over the bridge, past the school, post office and church. After passing under a fine bridge look for the ice-house in the wood on the left. Continue along until you arrive at a group of public footpath signs. Take the one on the right to do a 'u' turn and walk along a path through the trees close to the fence on your left.

2. This path leads to a stile into a meadow, follow the waymarks across the grass as you pass behind the Hall and lake. Eventually you will see a stile in the middle of a fence crossing the field. Follow the waymarks behind Mill Farm then drop down to the road over a stile in the hedge. Cross the road diagonally left then turn right at the footpath sign and over the bridge across the River Derwent and into a field leading to the tiny village of Wrench Green.

3. Keep straight ahead to join a tarmac road then straight on up the hill following the link sign for Cockmoor Hall. At the entrance to Slack Farm follow the footpath sign along the farm road. In a few hundred yards go right at the waymark up the hill. Keep following these waymarks round to the left then into a copse of trees to go right. At the end of the trees keep straight on through the gorse bushes and over the hill bearing slightly left.

4. Look out for the next waymark and a stile then down the hill and right through a small gate following the yellow arrow into a wood. Through the trees now to exit at the farm. This high ground is called Mount Misery and offers good views across to

Troutsdale. Keeping the farm on your left follow the fence round to the left. Once past the farm go straight on and over a stile through the hedge, down an overgrown path and onto a farm road. Turn right onto the road and follow it all the way without deviation onto the tarmac road.

5. Take the public bridleway opposite and climb up the hill following a wide track. At a small gate the route splits. Keep right here along the edge of the field following the arrow. The path soon crosses a stile into a field then heads diagonally right to another stile in the hedge. Bear left over the stile and head down through the bracken eventually reaching a stone bridge on the right.

6. Cross the bridge to take you past the farm to the road. Turn left here up the hill if you would like to take some refreshment at the Moorcock Inn. When you can drag yourself away from the superb ale retrace your steps back to the farm past the church and follow the road to a bridge over the River Derwent. Immediately after the bridge cross the stile into a field on the left. Turn immediately right and go straight up the bank side on a sometimes undefined path. Half way up you will meet a wide bridleway, turn left onto it to continue to the top of the hill and exit onto the road through a gate.

7. Go left now into Broxa village. At the end of the village where the road narrows follow the footpath sign to the right along a wide track. In a few yards go straight ahead and cross a stile into a field. Follow the track and its waymarks over several stiles and fields. After five stiles and one fence you are nearing the end of this penin-sula of land. Keep to the right near the trees now and look for an obvious wide track leading through a gate downhill. At the road turn left to return to your transport.

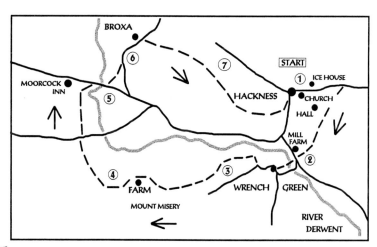

The ice house near the bridge in Hackness would have been filled with ice to preserve game and meat for future use at the Hall. Years ago most stately homes had these 'refrigerators' in their grounds, sometimes they were linked to the kitchens by a tunnel to prevent the servants being seen from the main house.

ROSEDALE ABBEY

Today, Rosedale's economy thrives on tourism and farming. But the area has been host to many industries in the past. The Romans brought weaving and pottery, the Cistercians built their Priory. The ironstone industry was rife as industrial Teesside expanded rapidly and became hungry for raw materials. The French even made glass here in the 16th century!

But what of the Abbey? All that remains is a buttressed turret which can be found in the village. If you stand with your back to the public conveniences near the Milburn Arms and look over the wall opposite you will see the turret across the field. Other remains will be found in the stonework of local houses. The Abbey was a Priory of the Cistercian order with 9 nuns and a Prioress. There were a few lay workers mainly farmers and shepherds. The Priory sometimes had twelve sacks of wool for sale annually taken from their large flocks of sheep on the moors. In 1322 the Scots raided Rosedale and severely damaged the Priory, so much so that the nuns were rehabilitated elswhere until repairs were carried out. It was occupied until Henry 8th called for the suppression of the monasteries in 1535 and the priory was destroyed.

FACT FILE
Distance - 8 miles (13 km).

Time - 3½ hours.

Maps - OS Landranger 100.

Start - Rosedale Abbey, GR 725960

Terrain - Moorland paths. Undefined in places over Northland Rigg.

Parking - There are two free car parks near the Milburn Arms.

But be early they soon become full.

Refreshment - There are two cafes and two pubs in Rosedale Abbey.

The Route
1. Start from the small car park behind the Milburn Arms. If full there is another park adjacent to the pub. Follow the public footpath sign through the gate at the rear of the car park. Cross the field staying close to Northdale Beck on your left. Keep following the beck crossing several stiles on the way until you arrive at a signpost. Continue straight ahead here following the sign for 'concessionary path'.

2. The path follows the river then after two more stiles you reach a bridge and a gate to a signpost. Keep straight on still following the bridleway sign. At the road turn right and in about half a mile immediately after a house used as a stable, turn right through a gate at the bridleway sign. Go uphill to climb onto the moor via a gate.

3. Take the left fork now and still climbing head for another gate onto open moorland. Soon you cross a wide track but keep on your narrow path through the heather. The track becomes undefined at times, even disappearing altogether. If you head for

the shooting butts slightly to your left you will come to a crevice, keep right here and follow the crevice which in winter could be wet.

4. This takes you downhill to a small stream. On the horizon straight ahead you will see mounds of the old workings. This is where you are heading. Cross the stream and you should see a narrow path winding its way through the heather. Follow the line of the wall on the right and when the wall bends to the right keep straight ahead to pass through the middle of the workings. The track then bears right to the road.

5. Cross the road taking the bridleway sign. The wide track soon forks, take the right fork away from the wall. Now for the tricky bit! In about a mile you will pass a pile of stones on the right. Then, in a hundred yards or so look for a wide swathe of grass through the heather leading to a gate in the wall on your right. If you reach a clump of trees on the right you have gone too far and are trespassing. You must turn right before the small plantation!

6. Pass through the gate in the wall and across a couple of fields to reach a quiet road at the side of a farm. Turn right here and walk along the road for about a mile where at a junction near a derelict farmhouse keep straight ahead, then in a few yards turn right at the public footpath sign. This leads through a pleasant wood rich in bilberries. Follow the obvious path along the edge of the wood and onto the moor, crossing two stiles and a gate.

7 At the road cross a stone stile and turn right then immediately left at the footpath sign. It is downhill now with scintillating views across Rosedale to the old mine workings on the other side of the valley. Pass through a gate and over a stile to arrive at a signpost. Turn right eventually passing over a large stile on the way to a farm. Go through the farm gate then left to exit onto the road. Follow the minor road to the junction and turn right to head back to Rosedale and the welcoming Milburn Arms.

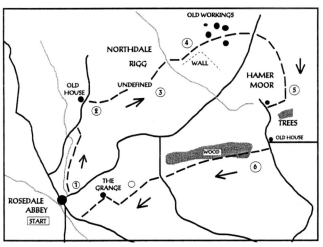

L ook out for the industrial heritage as you walk the moors, especially on Hamer Moor where there are numerous old workings. The Romans were around here, in fact a hoard of 3rd century coins were found at Hamer House. On the return journey look across the valley to the old kilns on the opposite side.

11

THE RUIN OF ST. MARY'S

The decaying ruin of St. Mary's church is the feature of this short walk. It is of Anglo Saxon Origin and there are some interesting carvings inside dating back to the 10th century. It seems there may have been a 'lost village' in this area. A mill still exists and was known to be working in 1200 AD. It ceased its useful life around 1930 when it was being used to generate electricity.

FACT FILE
Distance - 4½ miles (7km).
Time - 2 hours.
Maps - OS Landranger 94 or 100.
OS Outdoor Leisure 27
Start - Levisham. GR 833905.
Terrain - Firm paths but first section can be boggy if wet.
Parking - Levisham, please park sensibly.
Refreshments - Levisham, The Horse Shoe Inn. Personally recommended for good ale and food.
Public Transport - The North Yorkshire Moors railway runs winter and summer between Pickering and Grosmont stopping at Levisham Station. Telephone 0751 472508 for details.

- - - o 0 o - - -

The Route
1. Park carefully in Levisham village which is signed off the Pickering to Whitby road. Leave the village on the road you came on and shortly after the double bend follow the 'Link' sign along a bridleway on the right. At the bottom of the hill keep to the wide path straight ahead. To visit the ruins of St. Mary's Church take a detour to the left into the valley.

2. Returning to the route follow the wide track until it enters a field. Keep straight ahead now picking up waymarks occasionally as you pass through several gates and into woodland. Pass through a gate into scrub soon exiting via a small gate into the nature reserve of Hagg Wood. Exit the wood into a field then head for a bridge into another field opposite.

3. Keep to the right now following the line of the fence round to the right. This is Farwath. The railway buildings opposite are the home of a maker of besoms, a rare trade indeed! The N.Y.M. Railway runs alongside now but the path gently leaves it as it passes through meadows and gates into the forest. After a cool walk through the forest the path exits left through a gate onto a wide track.

Follow this round to the right then in a few yards ascend diagonally upwards to the right.

4. Where the path crosses a wider track bear left onto it and follow it to the road. At the road go right up the hill to return to Levisham village and a pint of Theakstons Hogshead beer. If you came by train, turn left where you joined the road to go to Levisham Station.

--- o 0 o ---

*L*evisham *is a pretty moorland village with the Horseshoe Inn as its centrepiece. It is the start of the walk to St Mary's church and gives glimpses of some of the most majestic scenery on the North York Moors. Stunning Newtondale was gouged out by water escaping from Eskdale at the end of the last ice age.*
It was in 1836 that George Stephenson opened a railway along Newtondale, although the coaches were initially drawn by horses. The railway was in operation for over 100 years until closed in the Beeching era. It was reopened as the North Yorkshire Moors Railway some years later.

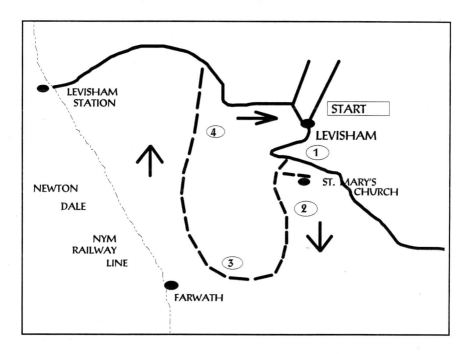

A CASTLE & AN ABBEY IN RYEDALE

A real treat this time, not one but possibly four superb monuments to visit! We start at the market town of Helmsley and visit the castle. Robert de Roos built a curtain wall on this rocky outcrop in 1200AD with strong, round towers. Defences were strengthened in the 13th century with the erection of two barbicans and double ditched ramparted earthworks. The remains seen today, damaged by a three month siege in the civil war, are impressive with a Tudor mansion with fine oak panelling being in good repair. At the opposite end of the walk is Rievaulx Abbey, built by white robed Cistercian monks in the 12th century. With its beautiful setting the abbey was popular and at its peak there were over 600 monks and lay brothers in residence. Rievaulx was dissolved in 1538.

If time allows you must make a detour and visit Rievaulx Terrace and the temples overlooking the abbey. The hunting lodge is superb with a magnificent roof painting and the interior set out for dinner.

- - - o 0 o - - -

FACT FILE
Distance - 6 (8) miles (10 (13) km)
Time - 3 - 4 hours (could be more if you linger at the abbey or temples)
Maps - OS Landranger 100
Start - Helmsley. GR 610837
Terrain - Easy paths
Parking - Helmsley near castle or market square
Refreshments - Helmsley and Rievaulx Abbey
Public Transport - The Moorsbus service stops at Rievaulx Terrace
Details from the North York Moors National Park. Telephone 0439 770173
Or from the Helmsley Tourist Information Centre in the Market Place

- - - o 0 o - - -

The Route
1. Park in the car park near the castle off the B1257 Stokesley road. Leave the car park and turn immediately left along a lane following signs for the Cleveland Way. You will see the castle on your left. At the end of the track continue along into a field keeping the hedge on the left.

2. Follow the path as it crosses a stile and goes left then right. Two more stiles confront you as you traverse these fields. Soon turn left through a gate into a valley then up the steps on other side following a fence past some old wartime foundations.

3. Exit towards Griff Lodge, cross the access track then continue straight on passing left of the lodge. Through a gate now to pass through the wood and eventually downhill to meet the road. Turn left here then at the bridge turn right to go to Rievaulx Abbey.

4. If you do not wish to visit the terrace and temples return the same way back to Helmsley. Otherwise after exploring the abbey continue on into the village following the road round to the right to meet the B1257. Turn right here and immediately right again to visit the terrace and temples.

5. To return to Helmsley I do not recommend walking along the busy B1257. You have a choice however. You can retrace your steps and return the way you came from Helmsley via Rievaulx Abbey, or you can catch the Moorsbus. Details in the fact file.

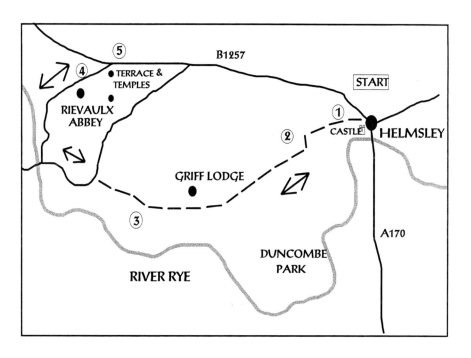

THE ARCHITECTURAL MASTERPIECES OF CASTLE HOWARD

I've cheated a bit with this walk as Castle Howard doesn't look like a castle. But I'm sure you will be impressed by John Vanbrugh who designed this magnificent house in 1699 for Charles Howard, third Earl of Carlisle in the days when large country houses were lavish status symbols. With some help from Nicholas Hawksmoor, the designer of the great Mausoleum, everything at Castle Howard was built on a grand scale. The building was started in 1701 and was still in progress in 1726 when Vanbrugh died. It was then overseen by Sir Thomas Robinson to its completion in 1759. Not only is the house a magnificent architectural masterpiece but the park around it was created as a classical landscape reflecting the influence of Greece and Rome.

FACT FILE
Distance - 6 miles (10km)

Time - 3 hours

Maps - OS Landranger 100

Start - Welburn. GR 718681

Terrain - Easy walking on well defined paths
and estate roads

Parking - Street parking in Welburn village

Refreshments - The Crown & Cushion Inn at Welburn
Cafe at Castle Howard if visited

The Route

1. Start in the village of Welburn, there is plenty of street parking near the Crown & Cushion. Set off in an Easterly direction then in a hundred yards from the Crown & Cushion turn left along Water Lane. When the road ends take the bridleway to the left of the gateway to a house called Primrose Hill.

2. When the track ends in field, turn right, following the hedge on the right at the old oak tree. Cross this field then go left through a gate following the blue waymark. The path falls down through a thicket to a junction of waymarked paths. Take the public footpath to the left and climb up into a wood, soon crossing a stile.

3. As you walk through the wood the Four Faces monument abruptly rises in front of you. Keep to the left of it then join a wider path taking you left again following the Centenary Way sign. At the end of the wood bear right through a gate following the CW arrow. On the left is the Pyramid and to the right the impressive Mausoleum looms into view.

4. The path soon meets a farm road, go left for a few yards then right through a gate following the waymark. In the distance is the ornamental bridge, when you reach it linger awhile and enjoy the magnificence of the view to Castle Howard on the left, the Mausoleum on the right and across the meadow to the Temple of the Four Winds, one of the finest small buildings in the country.

5. I must stress that no diversion from the right of way is allowed anywhere along

the walk to have a closer look at the monuments. The entrance to Castle Howard is at the Obelisk on the road and is worthy of a visit to explore the grounds and house. (It would be advisable to carry a spare pair of shoes with you)

6. Exit the bridge over the stile and head across the middle of the field up the hill. Bear left over the brow and aim for a collapsed stone tower in the left corner of the field wall. Leave the field over the stile adjacent to the large white gate directly in front of you. In a few yards take the less defined track to the left following the estate wall which leads past some very old oak trees.

7. Soon you meet a wider chalk road, bear left onto the road and shortly follow the waymark to the right. This leads to the road at Coneysthorpe. Left here then left again at the crossroads. It is about a mile to the obelisk, which is the entrance to Castle Howard.

8. A few hundred yards past the obelisk the gate house spans the road. Turn left before the gate house and head along the concrete road signed public footpath. Take the first turning on the right past the Pyramid, signed Centenary Way. Through the gate the path forks, go right down hill into the wood following the bridleway arrow. Follow the waymark across the field and return to Welburn straight ahead along the path past Primrose Hill to Water Lane.

W̱hilst walking through the grounds of the Castle Howard estate it is easy to become overwhelmed by its grandeur. Crumbling monuments appear dramatically in front of you and stare down as their privacy is briefly invaded. Whilst at every turn a new and even more imposing building appears. The crumbling Four Faces hidden in the wood, the Pyramid on St.Anne's Hill, the astounding Mausoleum to the north surrounded by its Doric pillars and the magnificent Temple of the Four Winds standing aloof across the meadow. Then as a trump card the view across the water to Castle Howard from the superb ornamental bridge. Castle Howard is second only to Blenheim in size amongst Vanbrugh' well worth a visit. The house and gardens are open daily from March to November. Telephone 0653 84333

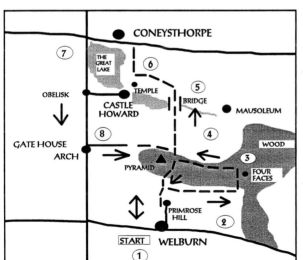

AN AUGUSTINIAN PRIORY

K̶irkham is an Augustinian Priory, although under the influence of one of its Priors it almost became Cistercian. In contrast to the white habits of the Cistercians the Augustinians wore black. They were named after St. Augustine of Hippo. Kirkham Priory was built in 1122 alongside the River Derwent. There is evidence of three churches being built within the Priory, although the third one was never completed. There are remains of some prominence here, the magnificent 14th century gatehouse is richly carved and the lavatorium is still to be seen within the grounds.

- - - o O o - - -

FACT FILE
Distance - 7 miles (11 km)
Time - 3 hours
Maps - OS Landranger 100
Start - Kirkham Priory. GR 735658
Nearest Town - Malton
Terrain - Easy paths
Parking - Small park outside the Priory
Refreshments - Cafe at the Priory in summer

- - - o O o - - -

The Route

1. Walk across the bridge over the River Derwent then turn immediately left over the stile onto the river bank. Cross the field then take the path through the wood which can be quite muddy at times.

2. Follow the river side path until you reach the first of two weirs. The path opens out into a field and is well marked and crosses some rather rickety stiles. After a mile or so you will see Howsham Hall on the opposite bank. This magnificent building is now used as a school.

3. If the river is in flood you will hear the roar of the weir at Howsham a short way ahead. As you approach the weir the path goes right over a footbridge then left down to another bridge which reunites you with the river bank.

4. Cross the stile into a field (beware of the bull) and aim for Howsham bridge at the other side. Turn right at the road then in ½ mile right again following the signpost to Crambe.

5. A pretty country walk through Crambe eventually takes you to a crossroad, turn right here following the sign for Kirkham Priory to return to your transport.

I is said that the priory was founded in memory of the son of the Lord of Helmsley who, it is rumoured fell off his horse and broke his neck at the site. There is a stump of a cross at the entrance to the priory where he is said to have come to his untimely end.

---o0o---

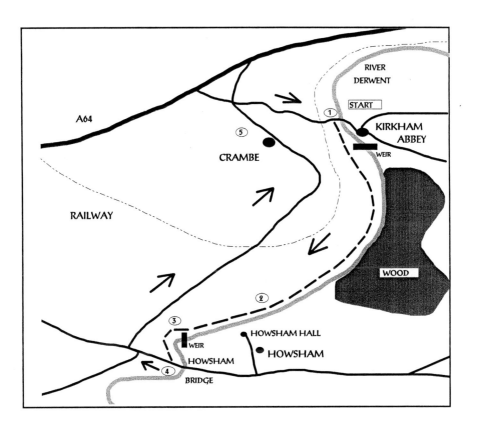

---o0o---

ROUTE 9
A SAXON MINSTER

*S*t. *Gregory's Minster is a fine church dating back to the 7th century. A stone slab was found here with the name 'King Oethilwald' carved on it . Inside the porch over the door is a Saxon sundial. It was carved out of the stone when the ruined church was rebuilt around the time of Edward the Confessor, about 1055AD. The inscription on the stone is the longest carved inscription in Anglo Saxon to have survived the ravages of time. Inside the church are more Saxon relics and even a coffin lid.*

--- o O o ---

FACT FILE
Distance - 3 miles (5 km)
Time - 1½ hours
Maps - OS Landranger 100
Start - Kirkdale. GR 676856
Terrain - Grassy paths and woodland track
Parking - Small park near the Minster
Refreshments - Kirkbymoorside

--- o O o ---

The Route

1. To reach St Gregory's Minster at Kirkdale leave Kirkbymoorside on the A170 towards Helmsley. After leaving the speed limit take the first unmarked turning on the right, keep straight on at the crossroads, over the ford and up the hill. Half way up the hill is a sign to the right for the Minster. Parking for walkers is here, at the entrance to the road, and **not** at the Minster car park which is for visitors only.

2. Take the bridleway signed through the trees up the bank, following the waymark arrow into a field. Turn sharp right here walking along the edge of the field keeping close to the wood on your right. Through clearings in the trees you will catch glimpses of St Gregory's Minster nestling below on the right.

3. At the road turn right down the hill to the 18th century High Cauldron Mill. When you cross the bridge you will see the cauldron on the left. On the right, unless Hodge Beck is in flood, you will notice the level of water in it receding. In fact it disappears through the beck's porous bed to reappear at Howkeld Mill further down-stream.

4. Over the bridge cross the stile on the right to take the forest road. Bear right at the fork then over the hill keep left on a path which eventually leads to a wood. Exit the

wood and cross the field heading for a bridge over Hodge Beck. Continue along near a fence to arrive at St. Gregory's Minster.

5. Leave the Minster to return to your car straight ahead. However there is another feature worth exploring near here. At the road where you parked turn left down the hill to the ford through Hodge Beck. Whilst climbing up the other side look left into a rock face to see a narrow slit about two foot high in the rock. This was a Hyenas cave and many relics have been found there.

--- o 0 o ---

*I*n this pre-historic cave have been found the fossilised bones of Woolly Rhinoceros, *Mammoth, Bison, Lion and many others. It extends three hundred feet into the white rock, varying from two to five feet in height. The bottom of the cave is covered in partially encrusted mud which preserved the fossilised bones so well that traces of gelatine were found in them. The cave was 'discovered' by Professor Buckland in 1820.*

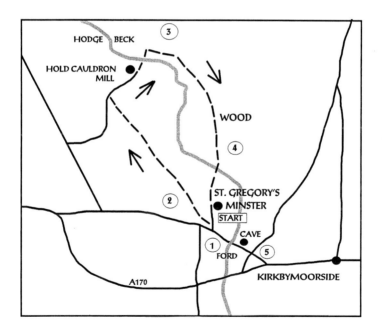

ROUTE 10

WARNING

Cliff paths are dangerous. They are slippery when wet and are subject to severe erosion. The cliffs near Whitby are very high. The walk is not advised to be attempted by anyone afraid of heights. Please take care and follow diversion signs provided where the cliff path is eroded.

THE GREAT ABBEY ON THE CLIFF

The foundation of an Abbey at Whitby was the fulfilment of a vow by King Oswy of Northumbria. He proclaimed that if he beat the heathen Penda at the battle of Winwaed in 655 he would found 12 monasteries and devote his daughter to the religious life. Hilda, Abbess of Hartlepool was given the task of setting up the Abbey at Whitby in 657, known then as Streonaeshalch. Hilda's monastery was inhabited by both men and women and its reputation grew so much that it became the burial place for royalty.

The Abbey was destroyed by the Danes in 867 and nothing much more is known about the site until 1078 when a monk called Reinfrid settled on the cliff on the site of the old Abbey. The monks had a rough time as they were set upon by pirates and local robbers, but they survived until 1539 when the Abbey was surrendered to the King.

The magnificent ruin on the east cliff today has suffered badly over the years. A terrible storm in 1763 felled the west wing whilst in June 1830 part of the massive tower collapsed. In the great storm of 1839 the wind blew down the south wall. Not only did the elements take their toll but the German Navy shelled the Abbey in 1914. The front was hit as was the west door. The building is now maintained by English Heritage and is open virtually all year round.

- - - o 0 o - - -

FACT FILE

Distance - 12 miles (20km)
Time - Take all day and explore the Abbey as well as
taking a lunch break at Robin Hoods Bay
Maps - OS Landranger 94
Start - Whitby. GR 903113
Terrain - Cliff path and cinder track
Parking - Abbey car park
Refreshments - Cafes and pubs at Robin Hoods Bay
and on return to Whitby

The Route

1. Start from the abbey car park then follow the sign for the Cleveland Way which

guides you to the coastal path by the Coastguard lookout and television mast.

2. Follow the Cleveland Way signs all the way to Robin Hoods Bay but beware of cliff erosion and take the signed diversions where indicated.

3. Explore Robin Hoods Bay at your leisure and try a pint in the Laurel Inn. To return to Whitby retrace your steps towards the cliff but this time take the sign for the permitted path onto the old railway track.

4. Cross the road at the caravan site continuing along the railway track until it finishes at the A171. Bear right here to walk on the roadside for a few yards then take the junction on the right for a pleasant walk back to the Abbey Car Park.

N̲o-one can visit Whitby without taking home some of Fortunes oak smoked kippers for tea. They are smoked on the premises and are absolutely delicious. To get there walk down the Abbey steps. At the bottom turn immediately right into Henrietta Street, lift your nose and follow the pong of burning oak and fish to the end of the street where you will find Fortunes.

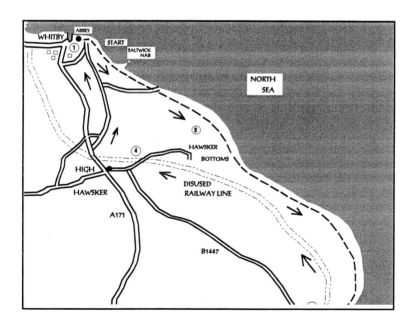

TRAILBLAZER BOOKS

CYCLING BOOKS
Mountain Biking around the Yorkshire Dales
Mountain Biking the Easy Way
Mountain Biking in North Yorkshire
Mountain Biking on the Yorkshire Wolds
Mountain Biking for Pleasure
Mountain Biking in the Lake District
Mountain Biking around Ryedale, Wydale & the North York Moors
Exploring Ryedale, Moor & Wold by Bicycle
Beadle's Bash - 100 mile challenge route for Mountain Bikers

WALKING BOOKS
Walking around the Howardian Hills
Walking in Heartbeat Country
Walking the Riggs & Ridges of the North York Moors
Short Walks around the Yorkshire Coast
Walking on the Yorkshire Coast
Walking to Abbeys, Castles & Churches
Walking around the North York Moors
Walking around Scarborough, Whitby & Filey
Walking to Crosses on the North York Moors
Walks from the Harbour
Walking in Dalby, the Great Yorkshire Forest
Walking in the Footsteps Captain Cook
Ten Scenic Walks around Rosedale, Farndale & Hutton le Hole
Twelve Scenic Walks from the North Yorkshire Moors Railway
Twelve Scenic Walks around the Yorkshire Dales
Twelve Scenic Walks around Ryedale, Pickering & Helmsley

DOING IT YOURSELF SERIES
Make & Publish Your Own Books

THE EXPLORER SERIES
Exploring Ryedale, Moor & Wold by Bicycle

YORKSHIRE BOOKS
Curious Goings on in Yorkshire
The Trailblazer Guide to Crosses & Stones on the North York Moors

For more information please visit our web site:
www.trailblazerbooks.co.uk